# Max and Charlie Help a Hero

**Never Too Young to Give Back**

**Help a Hero Books**

Story by Kim Roderiques and K. M. Ginter

Photography by Kim Roderiques

Illustrations by Giorgia Florena Shaban

**Max and Charlie Help a Hero**

FREEDOM

**Never Too Young to Give Back**

This book is dedicated to the men and women who have served
in the military and the sacrifices they have made for our country.

It is our hope that this book will inspire children to realize that they
are never too young to make a difference and help a person in need.

Kim Roderiques & K.M. Ginter

Front and back covers: Brant Point Lighthouse

Charlie opened his eyes and quickly sat up in bed. "Today's the day!" he shouted.

Charlie had just celebrated his 8th birthday and his parents finally agreed he could get a dog. School had ended and Charlie could hardly wait to spend his whole summer vacation with his new dog.

He jumped out of bed and ran downstairs to the dining room where his parents were enjoying breakfast. "Mom and Dad, we adopt our dog today!" Charlie exclaimed.

Charlie wanted a dog for as long as he could remember. His parents had told him many times that a dog was a big responsibility. Charlie promised that he would help feed and walk the dog each day . . . and give the dog lots of love.

After breakfast, Charlie said, "Let's go! Our dog is waiting for us!" Charlie and his parents piled into the family jeep and headed off to the MSPCA, the local animal shelter on Cape Cod. It was much bigger than Charlie expected.

labrador retriever
AGE 4

german shepherd mix
AGE 1

poodle mix
AGE 2

MSPCA, Cape Cod

The shelter had all kinds of animals: rabbits, cats, birds, hamsters and his favorite: dogs! "How do I decide which dog to adopt?" Charlie asked.

"Don't worry, I will help you find the right dog for your family," answered Mary Sarah, the director of the shelter. She walked with Charlie and his family, showing them the dogs available for adoption. There were big dogs and small dogs.

4

Charlie greeted the yellow lab.

"Hi, I'm Charlie," he said to the dog. The dog handed Charlie his paw to say, "Nice to meet you."

"Would you like to come home and live with me and my family?" Charlie asked the yellow dog. The dog let out a loud woof.

"Look, Mom and Dad," Charlie exclaimed. "This dog is so smart! He understands what I am saying."

Charlie gave the dog a giant hug and said, "I will name you Max. I know we are going to be best friends."

Max gave Charlie a big lick on the cheek.

They came to a yellow lab who seemed to smile at Charlie. "He's been at the shelter for awhile," Mary Sarah said. "This dog is a little older. He is four years old. Most children want puppies, but older dogs have a lot of love to give, too."

Charlie and his parents drove back to their house. Charlie was very excited to show Max where he would live. As the jeep pulled into the driveway, Charlie said, "Max, this is your home!"

Max's tail could not stop wagging. He was very happy to be with his new family.

Main Street, Chatham

The next day, Charlie and Max went to Main Street to see the 4th of July parade. The parade was so much fun. There were lots of people and dogs for Max to meet.

Max made two new dog friends at the parade: Oscar and Stormy. Oscar had black curly fur and Stormy had black spots all over. Max tried to count the number of spots on Stormy, but there were too many.

Charlie and Max sat down to watch the parade. Max let out extra woofs when the marching band went by them. He really liked the parade!

When the parade ended, Charlie said,
"Let's go for a walk; I'll show you our neighborhood."

The pair started walking down the sidewalk and passed the boat yard. There were so many new things for Max to see. Max liked looking at the boats. He had never been on a boat before.

They met Zaybo, a little puppy who was visiting Cape Cod with his family. Max let out a couple of woofs and gave Zaybo a lick "hello."

Mitchell River, Chatham

Fish Pier, Chatham

"Come on, there's more to see!" Charlie said to Max as they walked down the street.

They passed the pier where the fishing boats unload their catch for the day. They looked over the pier railing and could see a few seals playing in the ocean. A seagull landed on the railing and greeted Max and Charlie.

"Now, let's go to the beach," Charlie said to Max.

Max met a black lab named Coty as they crossed the foot bridge over the dunes. Max was very glad to meet another dog friend. Max and Coty exchanged some tail wags and a few excited barks.

Ridgevale Beach, Chatham

Cow Yard, Chatham

Charlie and Max played chase on the beach. There were several people on the sandbars digging for clams. It was a beautiful summer day and Max was very happy to be with Charlie.

FINISH

XIARHOS MEMORIAL FUND

8922

7345

6921

5511

SEAVIEW ST

5K ROAD RACE

Nicholas G. Xiarhos Memorial Fund

helping military families

Main Street, Chatham

The next day, Charlie took Max for a walk in the center of town. The street was blocked off from cars. "It looks like they are having a road race!" Charlie said to Max. "Let's get a closer look."

They kept walking. They could see a big sign that said "Finish" hanging over the street. A police officer was standing nearby on the sidewalk.

**Max and Charlie Help a Hero**

Charlie and Max came up to the police officer who smiled at Charlie and asked, "What's your dog's name?"

"His name is Max and I'm Charlie."

"Nice to meet both of you," the police officer said. "I'm Deputy Steve."

Charlie said, "Can you tell me what the road race is for?"

"The road race will raise money to help soldiers and veterans. It will also help their families."

"What is a veteran?" Charlie asked.

"A veteran is a man or woman who has served in the military," Deputy Steve answered.

"Veterans, soldiers and their families have given so much for all of us to have the freedoms that we enjoy in our country. Veterans are heroes. They deserve our respect and admiration."

Charlie smiled. He was happy the road race would help the veterans.

"Remember, you are never too young to give back and help a person in need!" Deputy Steve said.

Max let out a giant woof.

He agreed!

That evening, Charlie's mom started packing bags with clothes and dog treats.

"I forgot to tell you something, Max," Charlie announced. "Tomorrow, we are taking a trip to an island. We are going to Nantucket for the rest of the summer."

"You'll love Nantucket, Max," Charlie said. "We'll take lots of walks on the beach and I bet you will meet some new dog friends." Max wagged his tail. He could hardly wait!

Saquatucket Harbor, Harwich Port

The next day, the family went to the ferry boat that would take them to the island of Nantucket. They were greeted by the boat's captain at the dock. "Hello, I'm Captain Bob," the man bellowed. "Welcome aboard the *Freedom Ferry*!"

Captain Bob gave Charlie and Max a smile and said, "You two can be my first mates!" Max woofed.

As they sailed out of the harbor, Charlie and Max went to the front of the boat to get a good view. Max was very excited. This was his first boat ride ever!

Charlie looked at Max and said, "I know we are going to have a great adventure this summer!"

Brant Point Lighthouse, Nantucket

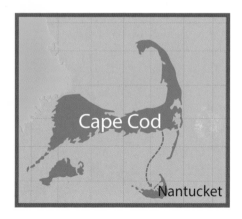

Cape Cod

Nantucket

The ferry sailed past the lighthouse and docked in Nantucket Harbor. Max and his new family walked off the boat and down the wharf to make their way to their summer cottage.

There were lots of people and dogs on the wharf. Max met two dogs who were visiting Nantucket for the day: Fenway and Zoey. He greeted them with a friendly bark.

Right: Straight Wharf, Nantucket

Charlie's family and Max settled in at their summer cottage.

Charlie and Max spent their days exploring Nantucket. They took long walks together around the island.

Old North Wharf, Nantucket

**Never Too Young to Give Back**

One day, Charlie, his parents and Max went to the center of town. They met a man who was sitting on a bench. His dog was wearing a vest.

"Hi, I'm Charlie and this is my dog, Max. Why is your dog wearing a vest?" Charlie asked.

"Hello," the man replied. "I'm Curtis and my dog's name is Nick. Nick is a service dog."

"What's a service dog?" Charlie asked.

Jared Coffin House, Broad Street, Nantucket

**Max and Charlie Help a Hero**

"Service dogs have a very important job," Curtis said. "They have special training and can help perform tasks for people. There are different types of service dogs. They can assist people such as veterans or people who have trouble seeing or hearing."

"Are you a veteran?" Charlie asked.

"Yes, I am." Curtis replied.

"A veteran and his service dog are a team. After training, a service dog is matched with a soldier who needs help. Service dogs help guide veterans through their daily routine. They also provide great companionship and lots of love."

"My dog, Nick, has become my best friend," Curtis continued. "Nick was named in memory of a brave Marine."

"I came to Nantucket for a ceremony that will honor several veterans," Curtis continued. "It's going to be held this afternoon. The ceremony is hosted by an organization, Holidays for Heroes, that raises funds to help military veterans and their families. Some of that money is used to train service dogs for veterans," Curtis continued. "Would you and your family like to come to the ceremony?"

Charlie looked at his parents. They nodded that it was okay. "Sounds great!" Charlie said.

Charlie and his family went to the ceremony. The veterans were honored for their service to our country. Two of the veterans honored had service dogs. The service dogs were given a medal for helping the veterans. Max really liked that part of the ceremony and he let out a few woofs to cheer for the service dogs.

After the ceremony, Charlie and Max said goodbye to Nick and Curtis.

Charlie remembered Deputy Steve's words: "Veterans are heroes and you are never too young to give back and help a person in need."

The Westmoor Club, Nantucket

Charlie turned to Max and said, "I think we should try to help a veteran." Max responded with a loud bark.

"I'm just not sure how we can help," Charlie said.

The next day, Charlie and Max took a long walk on the beach.

It was a very hot summer day.

"We need to think of an idea to help a veteran," Charlie said to Max.

Max woofed.

Steps Beach, Nantucket

Charlie gave Max some cool water to drink when they arrived at their cottage. Charlie poured himself a tall glass of lemonade and took a gulp. It tasted so good.

Suddenly, Charlie exclaimed, "That's it! I can start a lemonade stand and help raise money to have a service dog trained for a veteran!"

Charlie looked at Max and said, "We have a lot of work to do. We need to help a hero!"

Max wagged his tail. He was ready to help, too.

Mitchell's Book Corner, Main Street, Nantucket

The next day, Charlie set up his lemonade stand on Main Street. There were lots of people walking around town - some with dogs. Max made two new dog friends, Jameson and Murphy, who were staying on the island for the summer.

Charlie and Max worked at their lemonade stand every afternoon. Charlie always tucked a dog biscuit in his shirt pocket. After they closed the lemonade stand for the day, Charlie would give Max a dog biscuit to thank him for raising money for a veteran.

Each morning, Charlie and Max would play on the beach and swim in the ocean together. Max often met new dog friends.

One day, Max met a little dog on the beach named Gadget. Max invited his new friend to stop by the lemonade stand to see him. Gadget came every day to see Max.

The summer days went by quickly. Soon, there were only two weeks left in the summer before Charlie and Max would have to leave Nantucket.

'Sconset, Nantucket

Old North Wharf, Nantucket

One afternoon, Max and Charlie started to leave the cottage to go to their lemonade stand. Charlie's mom said, "You and Max have been working so hard at the lemonade stand. Don't you want to take a break and have some fun before the summer ends?"

"Mom, we are having fun, the best kind of fun!" Charlie replied. "Max and I meet lots of people and dogs every day. They are excited to help us raise money so that a veteran can get a service dog. If we reach our goal and help a hero, that will make us very happy."

Charlie's mom smiled and said, "I am so proud of both of you."

The next morning, Charlie counted up all of the money from the lemonade stand. He seemed a little upset.

"We raised a lot of money," he said to Max, "but I don't think we'll reach our goal before the summer ends." Max let out a big sigh.

"We need to think of another way to raise more money to help a veteran," Charlie said.

Main Street, Nantucket

That afternoon, Charlie and Max were at the lemonade stand. Max came over and put his paw on Charlie's shirt pocket where he kept the dog biscuit.

Charlie said, "I know, I know, Max, you'll get your biscuit at the end of the day when we close the stand."

Max put his paw on Charlie's shirt pocket again.

Max was trying to tell Charlie something. Suddenly, Charlie's face lit up. He knew what Max was trying to tell him.

"You're right!" Charlie exclaimed. "There are lots of dogs on the island. We should sell lemonade <u>and</u> dog biscuits. That will help us raise even more money!"

**Max and Charlie Help a Hero**

The next day, Charlie and Max started selling dog biscuits at the lemonade stand.

Max greeted the dogs with happy woofs as they arrived at the stand. Murphy, Jameson and Gadget were first in line for dog biscuits.

Charlie said to Max, "Tell your dog friends to spread the word. We are selling dog biscuits to help a hero!"

There were lots of excited barks and wagging tails from all the dogs so Charlie knew Max's message was getting out.

Soon, there was a long line of dogs and their owners getting biscuits and lemonade.

More and more dogs kept showing up each day.

**Max and Charlie Help a Hero**

Corner of Main Street and Orange Street, Nantucket

The summer ended and it was time to leave Nantucket. On their last day on the island, Charlie and Max counted up the money that they had raised over the summer at the lemonade stand.

Charlie let out a big yell. "Yes! We reached our goal. A veteran will get a service dog!" he said.

Max barked loudly in celebration, "Woof, woof, woof!"

Charlie gave Max a big hug. He announced, "We are a great team! We did it together!"

Nantucket Boat Basin

Max, Charlie and his parents went to the ferry to sail home that afternoon. Captain Bob greeted them at the wharf. "Welcome back! Did you two have a great adventure this summer?"

"We sure did!" Charlie said. "We raised money to help a veteran get a service dog!"

"Wow! Great job!" Captain Bob said. "I am so proud of my first mates!"

Charlie smiled and Max let out a happy bark.

Charlie and Max boarded the boat and ran to the top of the ferry.

"Max, we did it!" Charlie exclaimed. "We helped a hero get a service dog!"

As the ferry boat left the dock, Max gave Charlie a lick on the hand. He was so happy that Charlie had adopted him from the animal shelter. Charlie was his hero.

Brant Point Lighthouse, Nantucket

Charlie put his arms around Max as the ferry boat sailed out of the harbor. Charlie looked at Max and said, "I'm so glad we are best friends!"

Max responded, "Woof, woof!"

Max could not stop wagging his tail. His dream of finding a family who would love him forever had finally come true!

Charlie gave Max a big hug. They were both so happy to have helped a veteran in need.

**The End**

# Characters in "Max and Charlie Help a Hero"

Meet the real-life people and dogs who were the inspiration for this book ...

**Charlie**
8 Years Old

**Max**
Yellow Labrador Retriever

**Deputy Steve Xiarhos**
"Deputy Steve"
Yarmouth Deputy Chief of Police

**Mary Sarah Fairweather**
"Mary Sarah"
MSPCA Cape Cod Director

**Curtis Frye III**
"Curtis"
Cape Cod Veteran

**Bob Solomon**
"Captain Bob"
Holidays for Heroes Supporter

**Nick**
Golden Retriever Service Dog

**Coty**
Black Labrador Retriever

**Stormy**
Dalmatian

**Murphy & Jameson**
King Charles Spaniels

**Oscar**
Goldendoodle

**Fenway**
Silky Terrier

**Zaybo**
Corgi

**Gadget**
Maltipoo

**Zoey**
Havanese

# Never Too Young to Give Back and Make a Difference

If you ever wondered what inspires a child to go the extra mile, ask Luke Stringer. When the 11-year-old resident of Nantucket met a veteran, Luke's life changed.

The veteran, and Purple Heart recipient, suffered severe injuries in the Afghanistan war and is now deaf and blind. Because of his extraordinary service to our country, the veteran had become part of the family at Holiday for Heroes, an organization that honors families of war by embracing them with a retreat on Nantucket. The veteran told Luke that he needed a service dog specifically trained to help him with his complicated physical needs.

Luke decided to help raise funds for the training of a veteran's service dog. It was a great idea but Luke was challenged with the daunting task of reaching this goal. Luke, with the help of his close friends, decided to host a dog walk to raise even more donations.

At the annual fundraiser for Holidays for Heroes, Luke thanked everyone who had donated, announcing that $30,000 had been raised.

With Luke's dedication and perseverance, a hero will now have a service dog. Luke and his friends will have the honor of naming that dog. They are a testament to never being too young to make a difference!

Luke Stringer

Luke organized the dog walk to help a hero.

Luke and his friends fundraised at the dog walk.

Blue Buffalo Company, a Holidays for Heroes sponsor, donated dog treats to help Luke's event.

**Max and Charlie Help a Hero**

# Nantucket Holidays for Heroes

Holidays for Heroes was founded in 2012, by Tom McCann, after watching a Veterans Day celebration on the National Mall in Washington, D.C. Watching the brave men and women who were called to action to defend our freedom made Tom feel compelled to give back something for all that they gave for us.

## Holidays for Heroes Experiences

Holidays for Heroes Experiences center on Memorial Day, Independence Day and 9/11; three national holidays that honor America and the brave men and women who fight to preserve our freedoms. Behind every hero is a family who has loved, supported, and sacrificed. Holidays for Heroes seeks to repay each hero as a family unit. In so doing, we fill a niche that is too often left unattended. Our wounded Heroes and their families are hosted to a sorely needed, all-inclusive, Nantucket dream-come-true vacation retreat. We embrace each holiday together with Hero families the Nantucket way: parades and fireworks, fishing, sailing, clambakes, bike rides, group dinners with island families and new friends, and a tribute among this nation's most ardent political leaders and visionaries. Each Holiday Experience offers what is so hard to express in words: our deepest and most heartfelt gratitude.

Tom McCann speaks at a
Nantucket Holidays for Heroes event.

Veteran Jeff Lynch hugs his
service dog, Woody, at
a Holidays for Heroes event.

## American Dream Awards

From $2,500 to $25,000, American Dream Awards further education and training or small business start-ups for Heroes committed to building a future. Each grant offers a hand up, not a hand out. Grants for homestead handicap retrofits or down payments for a place to live relieve the pressures of providing a home for family, so heroes can focus on building their future.

## Service Dogs for Heroes

A newly created program, led by veteran B. J. Ganem, creates a national network that provides connectivity between worthy veterans, accredited service dog providers, and benevolent supporters. Highly trained service dogs are paired with wounded military veterans to improve the lives of these heroes.

Veteran B. J. Ganem leads the
Service Dogs for Heroes Program.

For more information or to donate, visit: **www.holidaysforheroes.com**

Bob Solomon, a supporter of
Holidays for Heroes, takes veterans
on a Nantucket boat ride on
Memorial Day weekend.

Marine Cpl. Nicholas G. Xiarhos

# Nicholas G. Xiarhos Memorial Fund

Nicholas George Xiarhos was the first child of Yarmouth Police Department Deputy Chief of Police Steven G. Xiarhos and Lisa Xiarhos and the beloved big brother of Alexander, Elizabeth, and Ashlynne of Yarmouth Port, Massachusetts. Nicholas had an enduring passion about serving his country and joining the military, which was heightened by the events of September 11, 2001. Nine days after graduating from high school, he entered boot camp and on September 22, 2006, he became a United States Marine. Nicholas served in Iraq and also in Afghanistan where his regiment supported Operation Enduring Freedom.

Nicholas died in Afghanistan on July 23, 2009 while going to the rescue of his fellow Marines in combat. Nicholas fought for the freedom of the people of Iraq and Afghanistan. He chose to make a difference in the world and was a true American Patriot.

The Xiarhos Family has created a fund in honor of Nicholas. The Nicholas G. Xiarhos Memorial Fund is designed to support local military families in need of financial assistance, wounded warriors and their families, and members of Law Enforcement.

The fund also provides support to many other programs including:

- The Nicholas G. Xiarhos "Does Most for Others" Annual Scholarship is dedicated to the male and female graduate who steps forward by living a life of service and does the most for others in need.

- Team Big Nick runs road races in support of charities all over the United States.

- Cape Wags for Tags is a special program in partnership with the Massachusetts Society for the Prevention of Cruelty to Animals of Cape Cod which includes in-home pet socialization and fee-waived pet adoptions for U.S. veterans.

Curtis Frye III, a Cape Cod veteran, received a service dog, Nick, who was named in memory of Nicholas Xiarhos.

For more information or to donate, visit: **www.cplngx.com**

Deputy Police Chief Steve Xiarhos founded this organization to help veterans, in memory of his son, Nicholas.

Veteran Curtis Frye III has developed a close bond with his service dog, Nick.

# mspca 🐾 angell

## Kindness and Care for Animals®

## MSPCA – Cape Cod

The goal of the MSPCA-Cape Cod is to function as the primary resource for animal welfare issues on Cape Cod. The MSPCA-Cape Cod cares for and helps over 1,500 local and homeless animals each year. Its tremendously successful adoption program includes dogs, cats, rabbits, hamsters, gerbils, guinea pigs, birds, fish and reptiles.

Animals are provided with the best medical and behavioral support possible and are never turned away as the MSPCA is the only open-admission shelter on Cape Cod. In an effort to focus on keeping pets and families together, the MSPCA has significantly increased offerings such as the food pantry, low cost spay/neuter programs, and rabies vaccination clinics. Cape Wags for Tags has launched a pet visitation program and adoption program for veterans. As more programs are offered, more needs become apparent.

The new facility, projected to open in 2017, will allow the MSPCA-Cape Cod the space to further develop programs designed to support all aspects of responsible pet ownership as well as expand its educational offerings for the children in its community including reading programs, volunteer opportunities, and eventually a summer camp.

Mary Sarah Fairweather, MSPCA Director, meets Max and Charlie.

The MSPCA-Cape Cod will be an environmentally responsible building with three distinct sections: Education, Medical Care, and Adoption. These three wings will represent the cornerstone of its mission to protect animals, relieve their suffering, advance their health and welfare, prevent cruelty, and work for a just and compassionate society.

For more information or to donate, visit: **www.mspca.org**

# About the Authors and Illustrator

### Kim Roderiques *(Co-Author & Book Photographer)*

Kim Roderiques, a long-time Chatham resident, is passionate about photographing people, places, and dogs on Cape Cod. Kim is the author of *Dogs on Cape Cod,* a coffee table book, featuring an extensive collection of dogs and scenic views from Provincetown to Sandwich. Her photographs have been exhibited in the New England region and published in national magazines. She was featured on the television show, *Chronicle.* Kim dedicates much of her work to the well-being of shelter dogs. Apart from her photographic career, Kim plays an essential role in the family business, The Trading Company, a fine clothing store in Chatham since 1976. Her new photographic book, *I Am of Cape Cod*, will focus on a cross section of people from different walks of life on Cape Cod.

Kim with her dogs, Hank and Rooney, photo: Marcy Ford

### Karen Ginter *(Co-Author)*

Karen Ginter, from Naples, Florida, spends the summers on Cape Cod. Her terriers were trained and volunteered as therapy dogs in the Cape Cod Companion Animal Program. Karen took the dogs into assisted living facilities and saw the magic that dogs brought to people by brightening their day and offering great companionship. Karen has also volunteered at the Big Brothers Big Sisters Program. She took her "Little Sister", who wants to become a veterinary assistant, to volunteer and raise funds at a dog adoption organization. Karen showed her that, no matter what one's circumstances are in life, one is always able to give back and help others, even at a young age.

Karen with Fenway and Monomoy

### Giorgia Florena Shaban *(Illustrator)*

Giorgia Florena Shaban is from an artistic family and has spent her summer vacations in beautiful Chatham since childhood. Primarily self-taught, the inspiration of her work comes from her family and pets, especially her dog, Oscar, who comes to the studio with her every day. Giorgia's art conveys the sweetness, love and humor animals give us. For the last 25 years, she has been working with her mother and one of her sisters at Tatutina studio in Pawtucket, Rhode Island, designing happy art and children's products. Dogs have always been her favorite subject and she is thrilled to have worked on a book supporting the MSPCA and honoring the veterans in the community.

Giorgia with her dog, Oscar

# Help a Hero Books

**Never Too Young to Give Back**

Look for more books coming soon in the **Help a Hero** book series.

*Read a book, help a hero!*

A portion of this book's proceeds are donated to help U.S. Veterans and the MSPCA.

Check out our star-spangled **Help a Hero** products at:
**www.helpaherobooks.com**.

Chatham Harbor

# Max and Charlie Help a Hero

Published by Kim Roderiques & K.M. Ginter

Copyright 2017 by Kim Roderiques & K.M. Ginter. All rights reserved. Published 2017.

ISBN 978-0-9978182-5-3

This book was designed and typeset by Nancy Viall Shoemaker of West Barnstable Press, West Barnstable, Massachusetts.

**Max and Charlie Help a Hero**